CHILDREN'S SERMONS
for the Revised Common Lectionary
Year B

CHILDREN'S SERMONS
for the Revised Common Lectionary
Year B
Using the 5 Senses to Tell God's Story

PHILIP D. SCHROEDER

ABINGDON PRESS
Nashville

Children's Sermons for the Revised Common Lectionary
Year B
Copyright © 1997 by Abingdon Press

Scripture quotations, unless otherwise noted, are from the New Revised Standard Version Bible, Copyright © 1989, by the Division of Christian Education of the National Council of the Churches of Christ in the USA. Used by permission.

This book is printed on recycled, acid-free paper.

Book design by J. S. Lofbomm

Schroeder, Philip D., 1964-
    Children's sermons for the revised common lectionary : using the 5 senses to tell God's story / Philip D. Schroeder.
        p. cm.
    Contents: [1]. Year A—[2]. Year B—[3]. Year C.
    ISBN 0-687-04996-2 (pbk. : v. 1 : alk. paper). —ISBN 0-687-01827-7 (pbk. : v. 2 : alk. paper). —ISBN 0-687-05577-6 (pbk. : v. 3 : alk. paper)
    1. Children's sermons. 2. Preaching to children. 3. Common lectionary (1992) 4. Lectionary preaching. I. Title.
    BV4315 . S335 1997
    251 ' . 53—dc21
                                                                    97-14948
                                                                    CIP

97 98 99 00 01 02 03 04 05 06—10 9 8 7 6 5 4 3 2 1

MANUFACTURED IN THE UNITED STATES OF AMERICA

For our children
Daniel, Kathryn, and Paul

CONTENTS —————————————

FOREWORD _____

Extension agents in Georgia relate this story about the possibilities for children to act as catalysts for change. It seems that the newly appointed cooperative extension agent was struggling to convince the local farmers to use all the new and innovative farming methods being touted by the University of Georgia. He knew that such methods and ideas would increase the size and quality of vegetable production for these farmers. The agent went from farm to farm trying to convince any farmer who would listen of the advantages of his "newfangled" ways of planting and fertilizing, but the farmers wouldn't hear of it. They weren't going to have an outsider come into their county and tell them that their granddaddy's way of planting corn wasn't good enough anymore. Like that old-time religion, that old-time agriculture was good enough for them.

Then the extension agent came up with a brilliant idea. Why not hold a contest for the children of the community to see who could grow the best produce? A Corn Club was begun for boys as they tried to grow the biggest ears of corn. A Tomato Club was started for the girls who grew, harvested, and canned the most tomatoes from their family's gardens. The competition had implications beyond winners and losers. Increased corn production meant more money for the family and more grain to feed the farm animals. Canned tomatoes provided many meals for families who had to grow their own food. Miraculously, many of the children began to reap more bountiful harvests than their parents, the farmers. Through their children, the parents were indirectly invited into learning the new processes and were not threatened by the new ideas, for these were "just kids." Soon the adults began to ask how they, too, could grow such beautiful produce, and in stepped the same cooperative extension agent to share these "newfangled" methods with the eager farmers, who had been transformed by the seeds their children and the county extension agent had planted. What started in 1917 as Corn and Tomato Clubs are known as 4-H Clubs today.

Using children as the catalyst for change is not a new idea. Jesus himself pulled a child from the crowd to make a point in his own process for stimulating renewal. His methods featured parables that shattered preconceptions and left his listeners holding the paradox! Applying this concept of children acting as agents of change to the worship setting can provide an avenue for congregational transformation. Children hold promise and can lead the way through the sands shifting beneath our feet and into the new paradigms emerging in front of our eyes, ears, mouths, hands, and noses. Too often children are seen as agents of destruction because they seemingly disturb the solemnity of the sanctuary, but their very presence often sets a community of faith in motion.

Significant and meaningful change within the church can take place only if we recognize the importance of tradition. Items of value are not destroyed or replaced, but are disassembled, reorganized, and then rebuilt into a new creation by the God who makes all things new using the same building blocks. Children, the most recently created, can help us in the learning process of rebuilding for the future.

In a recent interview, Bill Gates, the mind behind Microsoft, commented that children are not necessarily more proficient than adults, but rather more willing to learn. He said that adults for the most part are unwilling to put up with the several hours of confusion necessary to learn basic computer skills. Children, on the other hand, are in a learning curve all the time and are often "confused" at the proliferation of data. They abide momentary darkness in hope of light better than adults.[1]

An Objection to the Object Lesson

Worship is a mystery, not a collection of skills to master or a body of knowledge to be understood. It is an experience to be lived. We learn to worship by worshiping! Children learn to worship by collecting experiences of worship.[2]

The majority of modern homiletical techniques focus on the two-dimensional illustration, the word picture, as the customary approach to the preaching task. The preacher seeks to illuminate a text with examples, stories, and analogies that help the listener hear and understand the message of the text in contemporary terms. To illustrate literally means to light up. Light allows the object to be examined more closely, but it remains an object. The *object lesson*, the most common method for sharing the gospel with children, asks children not only to make cognitive metaphorical connections that are beyond their grasp, but also to remain objective, never becoming subjects of the gospel.

> *TRY THIS EXPERIMENT: Assemble a group of children in a room. Place a painting on one side of the room; on the other side, place a television playing a children's video. Where will the children gravitate? Your experiment will probably show that the shift from the still life picture to the moving picture has already occurred in the lives of your children.*

The children's sermon seems trapped in the age of the still life illustration or object lesson, the product of an earlier era. William Armstrong, author of the late-nineteenth-century book entitled *Five Minute Sermons to Children*, also struggled to find the most appropriate way to share the gospel with children. He understood that preaching to children took preparation but soon discovered that thirty minutes was too long for children's time! He finally settled on a five-minute children's sermon period that took into consideration his audience's attention span. His methodology is briefly summarized in the final words of his preface:

> Illustration is a necessity in all preaching (witness that of Christ), but especially in preaching to children. We all love pictures, but children love them most, and an illustration is a word-picture. An object sermon, if short and pointed, has a fine effect.[3]

Although Jesus did paint word pictures, it appears that he used far more than just object lessons to bring the gospel to life. Jesus was a multisensory teacher. He taught in ways that stimulated all the senses. Tasting, hearing, touching, seeing, and smelling were all part of his ministry.

Jesus helped those around him to taste and see that the Lord is good. He ate with sinners and tax collectors. He kept a party going by transforming water into wine. He taught the disciples by gathering grain to eat on the Sabbath. He broke bread and shared wine with his disciples who literally tasted the good news. Even after the Resurrection, Jesus asked for something to eat.

Jesus proclaimed the kingdom of God with his voice, and the people heard in new ways. He taught in parables that encouraged the hearers to listen, to reflect, and to respond. He invited people into the frames of his stories to struggle with the challenge of his words.

Jesus was constantly touching people while others struggled to touch him. When Jesus touched people to heal them, those around him claimed that in that touching, he taught with authority.

Jesus gave sight to people who had no sight and insight to the sighted. He pointed out scenes in their lives such as the widow's mite and told them to look at a coin to see whose picture was on it. He reminded them, "Blessed are the poor in spirit, for theirs is the kingdom of heaven."

Jesus was anointed for burial by Mary, Lazarus and Martha's sister. As the smell of that perfume drifted through the air, he taught of his impending death. (Jesus never seems to heal anyone who could not smell, but I suspect the lack of an olfactory capacity was a blessing in those days.)

Jesus used all the senses to communicate his message.

Swiss psychologist Jean Piaget argued that children actively construct reality out of their experiences with the environment rather than mimick what they encounter. Children live and learn rather than learn to live in the environment that is already in place. Everything does not have to be explained as it occurs, but as the child develops, she will begin to categorize and theologize about her experiences and draw her own conclusions.

In the first approximately two years of life, the sensorimotor period, children perceive only the existence of things that are within the immediate grasp of their senses. If they cannot taste, hear, touch, see, or smell something, it no longer exists in their world construct. This childhood stage features a sense of connectedness to all things. The child does not have a sense of where her body stops and everything else begins.[4]

This stage informs our human difficulty with affirming a God we cannot know through our senses. If an infant believes only in what she can sense, then are we not all infants in many ways? Children learn in this stage not by impersonal abstractions or arm's length study, but by an active physical interaction with the animate persons and inanimate objects in their lives. This stage is a time of exploring the world around them. Therefore, the children's sermon can be another opportunity for such exploration. It can be a safe time to learn to trust their environment and those around them. Children's sermons can respond to a child's search for things that are trustworthy in life. This first stage of learning, the lowest common denominator shared by all of humanity, can be the starting point for the children's sermon. If the children's sermon appeals to sensorimotor experiences, it will connect with all people on some level.

Object lessons may stimulate the senses of seeing, hearing, and touching, but there is little interaction with the object. At a church I recently visited, I listened as the minister showed the children a picture of an elephant. He asked the children, "How many of you have acted like elephants this week?" Blank stares were the response. A sensorimotor children's sermon on the same subject might have given each child the chance to behave like an elephant and discuss that behavior rather than merely talk about how elephants act. Object lessons allow people to remain objective, maintaining an "I-It" relationship; but Jesus set people in motion toward "I-Thou" relationships with God and one another. Jesus began a movement, yet many persons have sought to make him the object of their worship, an icon to be worshiped on the desktop of life. The life of Jesus is then used to illustrate a point instead of allowing his presence to be experienced in our daily lives. Christianity is not a still life picture, but a moving, spirited faith.

The Alternative—The Multisensory Subject Lesson

Multimedia can be defined as the confluence of written text, graphics such as photos, videos, illustrations, animation, and sound, such as speech and music to achieve a multisensory stimulation. Many multimedia computer programs have been labeled as "edutainment" products as the boundaries between learning and play have begun to blur. Computers allow for interactive learning when new lessons are constantly reinforced through the use of multiple senses at once.

Retention levels for all types of learning increase drastically when more than one sense is used to transmit the message.

> TRY THIS EXERCISE: Make a list of all the scripture passages you have memorized. Now make a list of all the hymns you know by heart. Which list is longer?

When words and melodies are combined, our minds retain more information. Multisensory children's sermons can help children to recall more of what has been presented, even though conveying factual knowledge is not the sole purpose of the children's sermon. Contrary to popular belief, entertainment for the children or the adults is not the goal of the children's sermon. Interestingly enough, entertainment has long been associated with passivity on the part of the one being entertained, but now entertainment is more participative than ever as people search for primary experiences. Children's sermons are more about experiencing the gospel for transformation and formation rather than for information or entertainment. Children learn by doing.

Children's sermons can be designed to develop relationships, establishing a level of trust between the leaders and the children while helping youngsters discover God in their own lives by hearing and participating in the retelling of the stories of God's people.

The same phenomenon seems to have found its way into many of our mainline Protestant churches as a congregation of spectators watch one person regulating the interaction. The sermon takes the form of a lecture, and the people are expected to consume the product being presented without response. In the silent print medium, there is no way of knowing whether or not you have, in fact, communicated your point when a person reads a document that you have written. Critiques and reviews of your presentation only continue the muted volleying between monologues. The shift in homiletics toward including an experience moves the people in the pews from observers to participants. By surrendering interpretive control of the presented experience, the sensorimotor children's sermon experience invites interaction between the worship leader, the children, and the entire congregation.

> *TRY ANOTHER EXPERIMENT: This time, instead of two choices, add a third dimension. Place a painting on one side of the room, a television with a VCR playing a video on another side of the room, and a multimedia computer displaying the most recently released Living Book CD-ROM in another spot. To which side will the children gravitate? A few children will still turn to the television to be entertained. Others will be fascinated with their ability to interact with the CD-ROM program, but only one child will ultimately be able to do so. Children sitting on the sidelines observing the multimedia presentation may soon opt for the television, since only one person can regulate the computer interaction.*

If we trace the evolution of the video game, the shift in the perspective of the player in relationship to the game suggests this contemporary movement from observer to participant. The first video game, PONG, allowed the player to manipulate objects on a screen in order to prevent a small ball of light from moving off the edge of the screen. The ball never came toward the player, but remained an object that merely floated back and forth across the screen. As technology improved, games such as Space Invaders gave the player the visual and auditory feeling that aliens were getting closer to the bottom of the screen, which is where the player's hands reside, but still the "I-It" relationship remained. Then innovative games began to feature characters that looked out of the screen toward the player. Actions were performed with the movement of a simple joystick and the pressing of various buttons.

Currently, video games have changed their perspective so the player is not merely a manipulator of pieces disconnected to his or her physical space. The player becomes one of the characters in the story. Racing games no longer feature tiny cars that move around a circular track fully displayed in front of the driver. The driver is invited to sit behind the wheel and drive down a road that opens up directly in front of him or her. The player not only moves the car, but the car is designed so as to make the driver feel the bumps in the road by shaking the steering wheel upon impact. This change in perspective moves the player from the position of an interested observer to an actual subject within the game.

Virtual reality invites us to a place where we become a part of the movement, a place where we can discover things for ourselves. Virtual reality, the experience of perceiving and interacting through sensors and effectors with a computer-modeled environment, is essentially about world building. Virtual reality creates places where drug researchers can assemble virtual molecules, where doctors can practice surgical skills on computer-generated patients, where astronauts can simulate Mars landings, and where architects can walk through dream homes. While many of these applications seem futuristic, virtual reality is already routinely used in airline flight simulators enabling pilots to hone their abilities to handle increasingly complex modern aircraft. Virtual reality provides a place for us to explore, to gain knowledge, and to practice skills we have acquired. With the advent of the multisensory experiences of multimedia and virtual reality, the dominant method of communication has shifted from the silently read, written word to the echoing and reverberating moving word.

During a recent visit to a virtual reality playground featuring an interactive exploration adventure, I found the most interesting aspect of the experience was not the game itself, but the manner in which potential players were taught the game. Recruits were herded into a room with a huge video screen where they watched an eight-minute movie. The movie portrayed other rookies participating in a real-life mission similar to our virtual one. Guidance was given only through this video parable of what happened to others in similar circumstances. The recruits were invited to become part of a continuing story by stepping into this virtual world.

Virtual reality in its current state has some severe limitations for use in the communication of the biblical text. As our earlier experiment illustrates, virtual reality often lacks a communal aspect and approaches the same individualism associated with the silently read text. I propose that the church embrace a *vital ritual reality* that takes the participatory stance of virtual reality and includes the virtues of the communal experience. As the community of faith gathers to share in the Eucharist, where the inanimate becomes animate, the story of our faith is not only retold, but also relived.

Vital ritual reality gives us the opportunity to relive the story with all our senses as we taste the wine, smell the bread, touch the hands of others, hear the words of forgiveness and consecration, and see the lifted cup and broken bread.

Our children and our churches need a *vital ritual reality* in which we can feel the power of the story of Christ with all our senses and thus celebrate a dynamic faith together.

Discovering and Designing Multisensory Interactive Children's Sermons

In the new system, the audio and the visual materials are not aids; they blend with the subject matter itself to evoke an experience.[5]

18

Take a deep breath and read the following passage aloud from beginning to end without stopping to catch your breath:

> For this reason I bow my knees before the Father, from whom every family in heaven and on earth takes its name. I pray that, according to the riches of his glory, he may grant that you may be strengthened in your inner being with power through his Spirit, and that Christ may dwell in your hearts through faith, as you are being rooted and grounded in love. I pray that you may have the power to comprehend, with all the saints, what is the breadth and length and height and depth, and to know the love of Christ that surpasses knowledge, so that you may be filled with all the fullness of God. Now to him who by the power at work within us is able to accomplish abundantly far more than all we can ask or imagine, to him be glory in the church and in Christ Jesus to all generations, forever and ever. Amen. (Eph. 3:14-21)

Reading this passage without pause communicates the connectedness of the text indirectly. Rather than declaring that, in their original form, these words of the Pauline Epistle were originally written as one long sentence, you, the reader, were asked to participate in one method of experiencing a text. This method transports the words off the written page into your mouth and into your mind. Multimedia presentations advertise the possibilities for a movement from the reading of a dry text to the reception of "an earful, an eyeful, and a mind full" of the ideas being communicated by the text. By your reading aloud, your relationship with the text has changed from observer of the silent print medium to participant in the continued life of the text.

Stage One: A Preparatory Posture

A close friend, Ginger Reedy, was attempting to make her home safe for her second child who was learning to walk. With her first child, Ginger had walked around the house picking up things and moving them to the next higher level so they wouldn't be dangerous for their older child, Sarah Linn, as she took her first steps. Unfortunately, Sarah Linn found innumerable items to explore and explode, in spite of her mother's best efforts. With this information from her history, Ginger took a new posture in preparing for her second child's adventure into walking. She got down on her knees, not to pray for the strength to deal with the child, but to inspect the house from a child's point of view. Ginger discovered that there were many things to be moved that she would never have thought of from her previous angle of vision.

The starting point for the preparation of the children's sermon is also a new posture, a preparatory posture. You might begin by performing a child's view accessibility audit of your sanctuary. Walk around the sanctuary on your knees to see what you discover from a child's perspective. I have yet to see a church with a children's pew where children can sit with their feet touching the floor. (Chairs from the children's Sunday school class would provide a temporary solution in some settings.)

Children are quite literally overlooked in many sanctuaries, and we do very little to dispel the notion that this is an "adults only" space. God chose to become like us physically in order to communicate God's love to us and save us. I propose this same physical incarnational approach to our sermons with children. Unless you turn and become like a child, not only will you miss the kingdom of God, but it will also be impossible for you to really connect with children.

Preparation for children's sermons is active, not merely intellectual. Children are noisy, messy, full of energy, and occasionally disruptive. Children enjoy moving, playing, and celebrating! They tumble in the grass, run down hills at full speed, do somersaults, and spin around in circles for no other reason than the physical activity and the release of energy.

Remembering the feeling of walking along a railroad track or a curb is not the same as going out and taking that walk again. We miss certain nuances if we rely solely on our memories of our childhood rather than take the time to participate in a childhood activity. Taking a preparatory posture brings us physically into a child's world. The preparatory posture re-members us into the community of children and helps us practice for the experiences to be shared with children in worship. Just as virtual reality provides practice for real-life situations, a *vital ritual reality* invites children and adults to practice their faith. Practice helps us move easily into actual situations and gives us tools to predict when something might go wrong. Practice is itself an experience that prepares us for other experiences. We practice our sermons for the adults—at least we are supposed to—but we don't seem to practice for our time with the children even when we do take the time to prepare.

We have applied the preparatory posture to the overall creation of children's sermons, but the children's sermon most often begins with the text. The Gospel lesson from the First Sunday of Advent of Year B of the Revised Common Lectionary is Mark 13:24-37.

What type of physical posture or movement emerges from this text?

> But in those days, after that suffering,
>   the sun will be darkened,
>   and the moon will not give its light,
>   and the stars will be falling from heaven,
>   and the powers in the heavens will be shaken.

> Then they will see 'the Son of Man coming in clouds' with great power and glory. Then he will send out the angels, and gather his elect from the four winds, from the ends of the earth to the ends of heaven.

> From the fig tree learn its lesson: as soon as its branch becomes tender and puts forth its leaves, you know that summer is near. So also, when you see these things taking place, you know that he is near, at the very gates. Truly I tell you, this generation will not pass away until all these things

have taken place. Heaven and earth will pass away, but my words will not pass away.

But about that day or hour no one knows, neither the angels in heaven, nor the Son, but only the Father. Beware, keep alert; for you do not know when the time will come. It is like a man going on a journey, when he leaves home and puts his slaves in charge, each with his work, and commands the doorkeeper to be on the watch. Therefore, keep awake—for you do not know when the master of the house will come, in the evening, or at midnight, or at cockcrow, or at dawn, or else he may find you asleep when he comes suddenly. And what I say to you I say to all: Keep awake. (Mark 13:24-37)

Possible Postures:
- Alertness, like a baseball player who keeps on his toes waiting for a ground ball or a child waiting for a parent to come home
- Asleep, curled up for a long nap
- Traveling, going on a trip, or a hike
- Yawning

The task of the preparatory posture is to encourage the sermon preparer to engage the text not only intellectually but also physically. The preparatory posture is a playful exercise. Too often we ask the children to think about waiting for Christmas or to recall trying to stay awake on Christmas Eve instead of actually creating the tension of waiting with the children as they gather. After a posture is identified, the leader is encouraged to take that stance during his or her time of preparation. Assuming a preparatory posture may mean taking a short hike, yawning a big yawn, or standing on your tiptoes. Doing this will probably feel silly at first, but it can be a valuable exercise. We communicate with children not only through our words, but also through body positions and body language. Children sense when we are uncomfortable with their postures. The preparatory posture becomes a plank from which to jump back into the text and begin the second stage of discovery.

Stage Two: The Experience

The question asked when designing the object lesson message is, "What object can I use to help me communicate a point based on the text to the children?" This method often falls prey to the "grab and stab" method of preparation as the worship leader searches the church in the minutes prior to the worship service trying to find a suitable object about which to make a point. Unfortunately, children will seldom retain the point that is trying to be forced upon them and will draw instead their own conclusions about the object in question.

If the intent of worship is to praise and experience God, the second stage poses the question, "How can I create an occasion during which the children can experience the story of God as set forth in the text?" We cannot give or teach faith to our children; we can only share the faith story as it has become our story and encourage the gift that is faith. The faith story is passed on by sharing, experiencing, and living the story together. Children and adults will grow in faith through shared experience and shared reflection.

While I was serving as an associate pastor to a church in Georgia, the senior minister was preparing to preach on "the pearl of great price." He asked me to compose a children's sermon from Matthew 13:45-46. It was not a lot to go on, but I tried to find a way for the children to engage in a search for a pearl of great value. Since pearls are usually found in oysters, I went to the local grocery store and bought a dozen oysters still in the shell. I rigged them so they were easy to open, and I forced a small pearl into one of the oysters. When the children came to the front of the church for children's time, we opened oysters together, looking for pearls. Finally, we opened one with a pearl, and the children were so excited that our search had been successful; we had found our own pearl of great value. They were not asked to recall feelings of searching and finding from their memories or told about my encounters with searching and finding. The children experienced the thrill of searching and joy of finding, which Jesus emphasized in Luke 15. These feelings can also be evoked by good storytelling and drama; but unlike what happens in storytelling, the children become a physical part of this story, and unlike what happens in drama, the children are themselves rather than the characters they portray.

I recall that particular children's sermon not for the idea I used, but for the feedback I received afterward. A father of two of the children at the children's sermon relayed to me the conversation that occurred on the drive home from the service. He and his wife were discussing the points of the senior minister's sermon when a voice from the backseat vaulted over into the fray. Their daughter recalled her experience with the search and added a new dimension to the family's faith journey. The children's sermon has a much greater value when seen as an integrated part of the entire service rather than when used as a break in the action to address the kids before they can be sent elsewhere.

The ritual dimension of our worship service is our faith community's theology in action. Ritual moves faith from the mind to the body as our ideas about God not only are thought out, but also become reality. A trip to the local science museum finds children running and jumping while learning about science. Discovering gravity and finding out about surface tension are not dull chores, but exciting experiences as the children are encouraged to drop things from various heights and make bubbles of all sizes. The cognitive development abilities of children are considered as this type of science education provides a playground for the senses. Learning about God can be just as exciting and experiential. We must begin to address children on their level instead of keeping them in the pew queue waiting for the time when they, too, can sit back and consume rather than produce worship. Liturgy has become the work of the clergy. Children, however, are not afraid to carry their part of the liturgical load.

Adults often see fastening their seat belts as a chore. My children see it as a game to test who can be buckled up the fastest. Now, it is not a case of whether or not to buckle my seat belt, but of how I can play this safety game with my kids. They have invited and encouraged me to do something that I may have failed to do myself. Children can play the same deconstructionist role for us in worship as they invite all of us into new experiences of God by their playfulness, informality, honesty, and willingness to explore.

When people recall meaningful worship services, they seldom use the language "I heard" or "I saw" the presence of God; rather, the sense of God is felt, experienced. We know God by participating in the text. Looking back to the first Gospel text in Advent, Year B, we ask the question, "How can we make this text accessible to children through their senses?" To find a multisensory experience, it helps to read the text with all the senses in mind. "Senses help us to think and react emotionally."[6] We taste the gospel at Communion, touch the gospel during baptism, and smell the gospel through the burning of incense.

Read Mark 13:24-37 again and make a list of what you sense from the text and what someone who was standing there listening to Jesus might have sensed.

- Sights: Clouds, falling stars, the gates, angels in heaven, Father, Son, Son of Man, darkness, doorkeeper watching for the Master
- Sounds: Cockcrow, keep awake, alarm, a ticking clock
- Tastes: Figs
- Smells: Fig trees, storm, winds
- Touches: Shaking, winds, gathering people, texture of fig leaves
- Feelings: Fear, waiting

25

Since we are forced to begin with a print medium, the Scriptures, sight and hearing are the givens for any sermon or children's sermon. The key is to layer as many senses within the children's sermon as possible, using taste, smell, and touch whenever possible. Even multimedia and virtual reality have not adequately included these senses in ways of which we are capable in the worship setting.

If we retain less than 15 percent of what we hear, oral sermons are like homiletical billboards posted all along the highway, seldom remembered or responded to beyond an immediate reaction. The task in creating a children's sermon is to discover what the children can do to experience the text rather than what they can be told about the text. Word pictures are no longer our primary means of communication.

When asked what they learned in school that day, young children primarily recount what they did, not what they learned. Children are doers! Their perceptions of what they do know are often distorted as one child in my first church recalled, "Mama, I do know my ABC's. It's just that my ABC's are different from your ABC's." Children learn the alphabet song and assume they know the alphabet. My children thought LMNO was a word, not a series of letters. Just because children can tell you they have learned something doesn't mean they can use it or apply it.

The intent of the children's sermon is to get children, as well as adults, thinking in new ways. Give children the text in a way they can understand. Allow them to discover the text and find meaning from the experience itself. Be willing to struggle with the loss of control as you are no longer making a point for the children or making points with the parents, but joining the children on a journey into the text and into faith.

Outline of the Methodology for Experiencing the Gospel

I. **Select the Scripture text to be shared with the children.**

   A. Exegete the text. Decide if the children can connect in some way to the text. Note: not all texts are accessible to children.
   B. If at all possible, use the same text to be used with the adults.

II. **Identify preparatory postures within the text.**

   A. Assume at least one of the postures you have identified.
   B. Move into the text physically in order to prepare for interaction with the children.
   C. Have fun; remember this is a playful posture.

III. **Search for sensory stimuli in the text.**

   A. List the stimuli as found in the five sensory categories:
      1. Sight
      2. Sound
      3. Taste
      4. Smell
      5. Touch
   B. Identify the senses that can be re-created in the worship setting.
   C. Identify which of these senses will connect the experiences of children to the text.
      1. Observe children in their interactions; listen to their language; taste the current fad food popular with children.
      2. Use all of your senses to prepare.

IV. **Bring the text to life with a multisensory experience.**

    A. Attempt to use three or more senses.

    B. Allow the children to participate rather than observe.

    C. Ask open-ended questions to help the children reflect on their experience.

V. **Link the children's sermon to the adult's sermon and the entire worship service.**

    A. Use the same Scripture text (if possible).

    B. Invite the adults into an experience.

    C. Discuss with the entire congregation any questions that emerged from the children's sermon.

FIRST SUNDAY OF ADVENT
LECTIONARY READINGS:
Isaiah 64:1-9
Psalm 80:1-7, 17-19
1 Corinthians 1:3-9
Mark 13:24-37

TEXT: Mark 13:24-37

PREPARATORY POSTURE: Set an alarm clock for a short amount of time, approximately twenty minutes, then take a nap! Keep alert!

EXPERIENCE: The feel of the alarm clock bursting into our dream-filled sleep is the sensation that you will attempt to create with the children during the children's sermon. The Energizer bunny pounding its way across an otherwise idyllic scene would have the same effect. Children will not understand the apocalyptic language of this passage, but the story of the man going on a journey can be relived.

Send one of the children to each door in the sanctuary, and ask them to be on watch for a man returning from a journey. Let out a yawn and encourage the other children to rest their heads on their arms and close their eyes. Arrange for someone with suitcases in his hands to burst onto the scene from an unexpected place in the sanctuary to symbolize the man returning from his journey. The choir loft provides an excellent hiding place in many churches. Having your beeper go off as you talk to the children might be a simpler way to stage an interruption.

Explain to the children that this is the beginning of

Advent, which literally means "coming." We are not really awaiting the birth of the Christ Child; we know when that happened, and it is scripted for December 25 this and every year. We do not know when Christ will return, coming on the clouds with great power and glory. Advent invites us to get ready for what God has in store for us. Ask the children to be on the lookout for Jesus during Advent.

SENSES: *Hearing, sight, and touch*

SECOND SUNDAY OF ADVENT
LECTIONARY READINGS:
Isaiah 40:1-11
Psalm 85:1-2, 8-13
2 Peter 3:8-15*a*
Mark 1:1-8

TEXT: Mark 1:1-8

PREPARATORY POSTURE: Walk along a straight line.

EXPERIENCE: Nothing seems to capture today's children more than the television commercial. Children often talk about things that are "Coming Soon," "Now Available in Stores," or "Coming to Theaters Everywhere." Using the prophetic words of Isaiah, the foreshadowing of the Psalms, and the words of John the Baptist in today's text, present a series of commercials telling everyone that Jesus is coming soon. Use members of the congregation or persons dressed as Isaiah, David, and John to act as celebrity spokespersons as they read today's texts. Place these commercials/interruptions at various places in the worship service, and then talk with the children during the children's sermon about the One who is coming. With preparation, the children themselves can present the commercials to the congregation.

Remind the children that John is Jesus' cousin. Pick one of the children to be John. Lay down a piece of carpet or plastic in one of the aisles. Make sure that it is *not* straight. Instruct John to straighten the path, and then encourage all the children to walk down the straight path back to their seats shouting, "Prepare the way of the Lord."

SENSES: *Hearing, sight, and touch*

THIRD SUNDAY OF ADVENT
LECTIONARY READINGS:
Isaiah 61:1-4, 8-11
Psalm 126
1 Thessalonians 5:16-24
John 1:6-8, 19-28

TEXT: John 1:6-8, 19-28

PREPARATORY POSTURE: Play a game of Twenty Questions with a friend. Practice phrasing questions that can be answered either yes or no.

EXPERIENCE: The text finds the priests and the Levites quizzing John as to his identity. Ask the children if they know how to play Twenty Questions. Explain the game to those who have never played, remembering that each question can be answered only with a yes or a no. Have an adult dressed as or representing John the Baptist visit the children's sermon. Let the children quiz him with twenty questions about his identity. After they guess his identity, let him explain who John was and tell them about Jesus. As he leaves, have him proclaim, "I am the voice of one crying out in the wilderness," "Make straight the way of the Lord." Tell the children to follow a straight path back to their seats. Our job, like John's, is to tell others about the Messiah.

SENSES: *Hearing and sight*

FOURTH SUNDAY OF ADVENT
LECTIONARY READINGS:
2 Samuel 7:1-11, 16
Luke 1:47-55
Romans 16:25-27
Luke 1:26-38

TEXT: 2 Samuel 7:1-11, 16

PREPARATORY POSTURE: Open a cedar chest or cedar closet and breathe deeply. Examine the collection of things inside.

EXPERIENCE: Bring in a cedar chest. Open the cedar chest and let the children smell the distinctive cedar aroma. Explain the purpose of a cedar chest. It is a place that keeps things safe. Tell the children about the conversation between King David and Nathan. David said that he was living in a house of cedar, and the ark of God stayed in a tent. The cedar chest will help the children understand what the ark was. It was a large box representing the presence of God that the Hebrews carried with them wherever they went. This is not the same kind of ark that Noah built.

Explain how God spoke to Nathan, probably in a dream. God told Nathan that the people of Israel would not have to wander around any more. They would stay in one place with David as their king. Then David would build God a house, too! Ask the children if they think God could live in this cedar chest. Pieces of cedar or cedar disks could be given to each child as a reminder.

Make sure that the children know that David was Jesus' great-grand father. Remind them that David was from Bethlehem, and what happened in Bethlehem.

SENSES: *Hearing, sight, smell, and touch*

CHRISTMAS EVE/CHRISTMAS DAY
LECTIONARY READINGS:
Isaiah 9:2-7
Psalm 96
Titus 2:11-14
Luke 2:1-14 (15-20)

TEXT: Luke 2:1-14 (15-20)

PREPARATORY POSTURE: Examine a nativity scene. If you have not already done so, unwrap and set up yours. Pick up each of the pieces, from the camel to the baby Jesus. Think about the significance of each character.

EXPERIENCE: Invite the children to the front of the church and begin to arrange them as characters in the manger scene. Have the children play the animals, the sheep, camels, cow, and donkey, complete with sounds. Then let some of the children choose wise men and women from the congregation to stand as those who brought their gifts to the Christ Child. Help them find a new mother to play Mary, a carpenter for Joseph, the shepherds, and the angels. When each character is in place, sing "Away in a Manger" together.

SENSES: *Hearing, sight, and touch*

FIRST SUNDAY AFTER CHRISTMAS DAY
LECTIONARY READINGS:
Isaiah 61:10–62:3
Psalm 148
Galatians 4:4-7
Luke 2:22-40

TEXT: Luke 2:22-40

PREPARATORY POSTURE: Fast for a day.

EXPERIENCE: Children will still be obsessed with the gifts they have received at Christmas on this first Sunday after Christmas. Invite two older members of your congregation to play Simeon and Anna. Costume them in first-century garb, and let them tell the children about the Christmas gifts they received as they realized who the child Jesus was.

To close, let the children tell about the gifts they gave at Christmas. Discussing the gifts they received will place the emphasis back on getting rather than giving.

SENSES: *Hearing and sight*

EPIPHANY OF THE LORD
LECTIONARY READINGS:
Isaiah 60:1-6
Psalm 72:1-7, 10-14

Ephesians 3:1-12
Matthew 2:1-12

TEXTS: Isaiah 60:1-6; Matthew 2:1-12

PREPARATORY POSTURE: Take a gift to someone who may have been overlooked at Christmas.

EXPERIENCE: Everyone is coming home to Zion, all the nations of the earth. Children understand coming home, especially after a busy holiday season of traveling. Invite the boys to the front of the church as "sons from far away." Then ask parents or others close by to come forward carrying the girls in their arms as "daughters carried in their arms." Discuss the feelings of being away and coming home. Read the Gospel passage from Matthew. Answer any questions the children might have about the story. Instruct all to return to their seats by a different path from the one they chose to come to the front, following the wise men's example of returning by another road.

SENSES: *Hearing, sight, and touch*

BAPTISM OF THE LORD (First Sunday After the Epiphany)
LECTIONARY READINGS:
Genesis 1:1-5
Psalm 29
Acts 19:1-7
Mark 1:4-11

TEXT: Mark 1:4-11

PREPARATORY POSTURE: Eat something unusual that you wouldn't normally eat.

EXPERIENCE: Children are fascinated with the portrait of John the Baptist in Mark. Dress one child as John with the following items of clothing, two of which may be found on people in the congregation:
1. A camel's hair coat
2. A leather girdle or belt
3. Sandals

Then give all the children a taste of locust and wild honey. Comb honey is perfect for this. The locusts might be represented by minipopcorn or rice cakes. Have enough for all the children to taste.

Ask John to announce the sermon for the day or introduce his cousin to the congregation.

SENSES: *Hearing, sight, touch, smell, and taste*

SECOND SUNDAY AFTER THE EPIPHANY
LECTIONARY READINGS:
1 Samuel 3:1-10 (11-20)
Psalm 139:1-6, 13-18
1 Corinthians 6:12-20
John 1:43-51

TEXT: 1 Samuel 3:1-10 (11-20)

PREPARATORY POSTURE: Make a recording of your voice and listen to it.

EXPERIENCE: Retell the story of Samuel's calling. Let the children participate in the role of Samuel. Call to the children, "Samuel! Samuel!" Let them respond, "Here I am!" Have them run to someone playing Eli and say, "Here I am, for you called me." Eli denies calling Samuel and sends the children back to sleep. Repeat the scene two more times. The last time, Eli tells Samuel it is God calling him. Ask the children to describe what they think God sounds like. Ask the rest of the congregation for ideas. Point out the images in Scripture such as the still small voice. For additional ideas on what God sounds like, read Tom Troeger's book *The Parable of Ten Preachers*.

A balloon with words written on it might be batted around and kept aloft as you recall that none of Samuel's words "fell to the ground."

SENSES: *Hearing, sight, and touch*

THIRD SUNDAY AFTER THE EPIPHANY
LECTIONARY READINGS:
Jonah 3:1-5, 10
Psalm 62:5-12
1 Corinthians 7:29-31
Mark 1:14-20

TEXT: Mark 1:14-20

PREPARATORY POSTURE: Visit someone at his or her workplace.

EXPERIENCE: The children's carnival fishing pond makes a great backdrop for this text. A place in the sanctuary such as the choir loft might make a perfect fishing hole. If not, tie a piece of rope between two sticks and drape a blue bedsheet over the rope. Hide someone behind the sheet. Have the children cast little fishing poles made of sticks and string with clothespins on the end of their lines over the top of the sheet into the pond. The hidden person then attaches paper fish to the clothespins and gives a tug. At first, let very few fish be caught, then tell them that Jesus invited his disciples to fish for people. Send the children out in the congregation to fish. See if they can catch any people for Christ.

SENSES: *Hearing, sight, and touch*

FOURTH SUNDAY AFTER THE EPIPHANY
LECTIONARY READINGS:
Deuteronomy 18:15-20
Psalm 111
1 Corinthians 8:1-13
Mark 1:21-28

TEXT: Deuteronomy 18:15-20

PREPARATORY POSTURE: Climb a mountain. Take a hike.

EXPERIENCE: God tells Moses that he will put his words in the mouth of the prophet. Ask the children, "What kinds of words do you think God would put into our mouths?" Pour out a box of Alpha-bits cereal onto a large tray. Help the children form words such as *God, Jesus, love, Lord,* and *Christ.* Then literally put these words in the children's mouths so they may commune on God's Word for themselves.

SENSES: *Hearing, taste, sight, and touch*

FIFTH SUNDAY AFTER THE EPIPHANY
LECTIONARY READINGS:
Isaiah 40:21-31
Psalm 147:1-11, 20c

1 Corinthians 9:16-23
Mark 1:29-39

TEXT: 1 Corinthians 9:16-23

PREPARATORY POSTURE: Go to an auction. Try to talk like an auctioneer.

EXPERIENCE: In order to explain Paul's words in verse 18 that the gospel is free of charge, hand each of the children a few dollars worth of play money. Ask them if they know what an auction is and explain it to those who do not know. An auction is a way for us to put value on things. With the help of an experienced auctioneer, auction off a few things the children might be interested in. Take the play money as payment. Then offer a symbol of good news such as a Bible or a cross and continue the auction. You may want to plant some adults to help with the bidding. Have the bidding go as high as anyone's money can go, and then say that you cannot sell that symbol of the good news.

God's love for us in Christ is not for sale, it can only be given away. Give each child a symbol of the good news and let them keep the play money. This can also be set up as the "Price Is Right" as the children try to guess the prices of various items, the last one being a sign with the word LOVE on it. I did this one Easter and the children tried to get closest without going over for each prize until I got to LOVE. One little boy said, "Aw, you can't put a price on love." I could not have asked for a better answer. God's gifts, like those offered in the Isaiah text for today are priceless.

SENSES: *Hearing and sight*

SIXTH SUNDAY AFTER THE EPIPHANY
LECTIONARY READINGS:
2 Kings 5:1-14
Psalm 30
1 Corinthians 9:24-27
Mark 1:40-45

TEXT: 2 Kings 5:1-14

PREPARATORY POSTURE: Immerse yourself in a pool seven times. Rip a piece of clothing and then mend it.

EXPERIENCE: There are many pieces of the story of the healing of Naaman that do not need to be repeated for children, but they will enjoy this story of the healing of a great warrior and a king who rips his clothes. Ask them about ripping their clothes and the consequences. Explain the concept of rending one's clothes when in grief or distress. Select children to play the roles of Naaman, Elisha, a young girl held captive, a messenger, and the kings of Israel and Aram. Dress the king of Israel in something that can be ripped. Begin by telling the children that Naaman had a skin disease even though he was a mighty warrior. Help the children act out the rest of the story. Point out that the king of Israel thinks that the king of Aram is trying to pick a fight. The importance of following instructions can also be illustrated as Naaman is required to immerse himself in the Jordan seven times. Elisha's unwillingness to accept payment for this healing might also be discussed.

SENSES: *Hearing, touch, and sight*

LAST SUNDAY AFTER THE EPIPHANY
(Transfiguration Sunday)
LECTIONARY READINGS:
2 Kings 2:1-12
Psalm 50:1-6
2 Corinthians 4:3-6
Mark 9:2-9

TEXT: 2 Kings 2:1-12

PREPARATORY POSTURE: Take a hike up a nearby hill; come back down the hill as quickly as you can.

EXPERIENCE: In the Old Testament lesson we find Elijah taking his successor, Elisha, on a farewell tour. Perhaps the yoke of obedience, the mantle of service, can be seen as a new standard of success. Use the pastor's stoles to explain what a mantle is and how a mantle was passed on from one generation to the next. Dramatically retell the story of Elijah parting the waters of the Jordan and then being taken up into heaven by a whirlwind, a chariot of fire, and horses of fire. Tell the children about Elisha's sadness expressed by the tearing of his clothes. Then expand the pericope to include verses 13 and 14, pointing out that when Elijah drops his mantle, Elisha picks it up in order to continue the work that Elijah was doing. Drop a mantle or stole on the floor or the altar. Help the children find ways in which they can serve God as each one is given the opportunity to pick up the mantle that was dropped.

At the end of the service, drop your stole on the floor. If someone comes to pick up that mantle of ministry, begin an altar call that involves yoking people for the ministries to which they are called.

Another idea: Jesus instructs Peter, James, and John to

tell no one. Illustrate how hard this is by blowing up a balloon until it bursts. Filled with the joy of the experience, a person finds it hard to keep the secret of God's love inside without bursting. The good news is hard to contain!

SENSES: *Hearing, sight, and touch*

FIRST SUNDAY IN LENT
LECTIONARY READINGS:
Genesis 9:8-17
Psalm 25:1-10
1 Peter 3:18-22
Mark 1:9-15

TEXT: Mark 1:9-15

PREPARATORY POSTURE: Take a walk along a curb or a railroad track.

EXPERIENCE: The wilderness is found at the edge, the frontier, of civilization. Find an edge like the edge of a step in your sanctuary that you and the children can stand along. It doesn't have to be the traditional spot for the children's sermon. Have the children stand close to the edge of the step and then move closer and closer and closer. Some will lose their balance; others will hang on with their heels. Keep them moving closer until only one person is left on the step. Children will then know that it is difficult to stand on an edge as they have just done or to walk along the edge as they have probably experienced by walking a railroad track or a curb. We all eventually lose our balance. When we get to the edge, we are tempted to venture out too far. John the Baptist tells us we can repent, or turn around, when we get too close to the edges in our lives and not lose our balance. Jesus went out to the edge of his world and was tempted, but relied on God for his balance and did not fall.

Another idea: Have calendars for each child, whether Lenten or from a local business. Give children the chance to count the days between Ash Wednesday and Easter. They will find forty-six rather than forty days. Perhaps they will be able to resolve the discrepancy. (Sundays are excluded and are to be days of celebration.) The Marcan text mentions Jesus' forty days in the wilderness, and this can be highlighted for the children for its connection to the length of Lent.

SENSES: *Hearing, sight, and touch*

SECOND SUNDAY IN LENT
LECTIONARY READINGS:
Genesis 17:1-7, 15-16
Psalm 22:23-31
Romans 4:13-25
Mark 8:31-38

TEXT: Mark 8:31-38

PREPARATORY POSTURE: Pick up a cross that is especially meaningful to you.

EXPERIENCE: Find or make a large cross that is too heavy for any child to lift or carry individually. (I would say, "Watch for splinters!" but splinters might make the point even better than we can.) Some churches use special Lenten crosses in the sanctuary, and these can be used with care. Lay the cross down on the floor, and ask one child to pick up the cross. See how the child does. Other children may volunteer to help or can be encouraged to do so until they can pick up the cross. Read the verse from the Marcan passage, "If any want to become my followers, let them deny themselves and take up their cross and follow me." Allow the children to react to the meaning of the statement. This exercise shows children that they cannot do it alone and that others can and will help them as they struggle to follow Jesus.

Another idea: Celebrate this Sunday as Cross Sunday and invite people to bring their favorite crosses with them to church. Take time in the worship service for individuals to share the significance of the cross with others.

SENSES: *Hearing, sight, and touch*

THIRD SUNDAY IN LENT
LECTIONARY READINGS:
Exodus 20:1-17
Psalm 19
1 Corinthians 1:18-25
John 2:13-22

TEXT: John 2:13-22

PREPARATORY POSTURE: Take some time to play with a pet—yours or someone else's.

EXPERIENCE: Fill a card table with coins and stuffed animals, sheep, cows, and doves if possible. Describe what Jesus saw in the Temple and what made him angry. Then flip over the table, letting all the stuffed animals and the coins fall to the floor. This can be a dramatic moment as you push the limits of what some would call appropriate behavior for a sanctuary. Allow the children to share their reactions to Jesus' actions and your actions. Maybe you want to find out about a time when they were angry. Do not be tempted to clean up the mess. Leave the scattered toys and coins on the floor as a visual reminder for the rest of the service.

SENSES: *Hearing and sight*

FOURTH SUNDAY IN LENT
LECTIONARY READINGS:
Numbers 21:4-9
Psalm 107:1-3, 17-22
Ephesians 2:1-10
John 3:14-21

TEXTS: Numbers 21:4-9; John 3:14-21

PREPARATORY POSTURE: Climb a tree! Take a walk through the woods or through a wooded area.

EXPERIENCE: Talk about going into the wilderness or woods without any food or water. Eventually, what happens? We get hungry and thirsty and begin to complain. That was just what the Hebrew children did. They complained, and God sent poisonous snakes that bit people, and many Israelites died. The people came to Moses and asked him to talk to God about the snakes. So Moses prayed for the people, and the Lord said to Moses, "Make a poisonous serpent, and set it on a pole." Have a pole, a stick, a plastic snake, and some masking tape available. Help the children make a serpent on a pole in the shape of a cross. Have the children carry the pole around the sanctuary and tell people to look at it and live. Then make the transition from the lifted snake to Jesus lifted up on a cross. The lifted snake helped people who were bitten by snakes; the lifted Jesus helps us all.

Another idea: Have a bedsheet available and write "John 3:16" on it, or ask a member of the congregation or the choir to hold up a "John 3:16" bedsheet like banners seen at sporting events. When the children notice the banner, talk with them about the text and why someone would go to sporting events and hold up similar signs.

SENSES: *Touch, hearing, and sight*

FIFTH SUNDAY IN LENT
LECTIONARY READINGS:
Jeremiah 31:31-34
Psalm 51:1-12
Hebrews 5:5-10
John 12:20-33

TEXT: Jeremiah 31:31-34

PREPARATORY POSTURE: Cut out a paper heart and write the laws of God that you strive to live by on that heart.

EXPERIENCE: **For small churches:** Do not invite the children to come forward. Instead, go to each child individually and lead each one by the hand to the place where the children's moments are usually held. Ask the children the following: Whom do you hold hands with? Why is holding hands important? When is holding hands important?

Discuss the children's answers. Did they willingly take your hand? Why? Why not? Read from the Jeremiah text how God took the people by the hand and led them out of Egypt.

For large churches: Make enough paper hearts for each child to have one. Have parents lead their children by the hand to the children's moments. Give a heart and a pencil to each parent. Talk about the rules by which God wants us to live. Ask the children what rules God wants us to live by. Instruct the parents to write one of the rules on the child's paper heart. Then encourage the children to place the paper heart close to their hearts, even inside their clothes, as they put God's law within them. Hearts with preprinted laws such as the Ten Commandments could also be used to save time.

SENSES: *Hearing, sight, and touch*

PASSION/PALM SUNDAY
LECTIONARY READINGS:
Isaiah 50:4-9*a*
Psalm 31:9-16
Philippians 2:5-11
Mark 11:1-11; Mark 14:1–15:47

TEXTS: Mark 11:1-11; 14:1–15:47

PREPARATORY POSTURE: Allow someone to blindfold you, then spend some time moving around blindfolded. A journey through the sanctuary blindfolded might be revealing.

EXPERIENCE: Tell the children that some people spit on Jesus. Others hit him, and then they blindfolded him. Blindfold one of the children. Be sure to tell the other children they cannot hit or spit upon this child. Spin the child around as you would for a Pin the Tail on the Donkey game. Then ask him or her questions about the other children as you explain why the people yelled, "Prophesy." Questions might include, "What is Tommy wearing?" and "What color are the altar clothes today?" Let them talk about how Jesus must have felt when these things happened to him. Some children may have been spit upon; others have been beaten up. You may hear some stories you do not want to hear, but Passion Sunday and Holy Week are full of those times!

SENSES: *Hearing, sight, and touch*

EASTER DAY
LECTIONARY READINGS:
Acts 10:34-43
Psalm 118:1-2, 14-24
1 Corinthians 15:1-11
Mark 16:1-8 or John 20:1-18

Text: Mark 16:1-8

PREPARATORY POSTURE: Walk though a garden at daybreak.

EXPERIENCE: Although there are many situations when children fight to be first, there are plenty of occasions when one hears, "You go first!" "No, you go first." Someone has to find the courage to go first. My generation had Mikey, the little boy from the Life cereal commercials who was willing to go first and try something new. As the women walked to the tomb, they were trying to decide how to get into the tomb, not who was going to go in first. The men stayed at home, probably telling the women, "You go first!" There is a sense of courage among these women who go to the tomb, but they find the tomb empty and flee in fear.

Verse 8 tells us, "They went out and fled from the tomb, for terror and amazement had seized them; and they said nothing to anyone, for they were afraid." Children will tell you some of the things they are afraid of. Let them know that God is willing to go first so we don't have to be scared. God goes first, and we are to follow God. We say, "You go first" and God says, "Okay, follow me."

SENSES: *Touch, hearing, and sight*

SECOND SUNDAY OF EASTER
LECTIONARY READINGS:
Acts 4:32-35
Psalm 133
1 John 1:1–2:2
John 20:19-31

TEXT: John 20:19-31

PREPARATORY POSTURE: Take a moment to examine the scars and scabs on your body and remember what caused the markings. Look at your own hands and side and discover how the years have changed their appearance.

EXPERIENCE: Children love to tell about their scrapes, hurts, ouches, and boo-boos. My children are fascinated with Band-Aids, which must be used on anything that even resembles a break in the skin. Children can tell us more about open wounds than any congregation would ever want to hear, so ask them to show their wounds. Children seem to think the wounds make the hurt more real! Seeing the scab makes the story of how you got the scrape credible. And the words of Thomas echo, "Unless I see the mark of the nails in his hands, and put my finger in the mark of the nails and my hand in his side, I will not believe." Placing a red dot on each child's palm would be a helpful reminder of the stigmata. Children are all too familiar with hurt and pain, and we should not shy away from the talk of blood and wounds for their benefit. Teach the children the name of Jesus in sign language by taking the right index finger and placing it into the palm of the left hand as if into a wound and then repeating the process with the left index finger and the right palm.

SENSES: *Touch, hearing, and sight*

THIRD SUNDAY OF EASTER
LECTIONARY READINGS:
Acts 3:12-19
Psalm 4
1 John 3:1-7
Luke 24:36b-48

TEXT: Luke 24:36b-48

PREPARATORY POSTURE: Go fishing. Visit an aquarium or local pet store and watch the fish. Eat fish for your evening meal and read the Gospel text to those eating with you.

EXPERIENCE: Ask the children, "What makes you hungry?" The smell of food will often make us hungry. Prepare a piece of broiled fish to share with the children and let them smell it. While they are busy smelling, catch them off guard by having someone speak the words "Peace be with you" over your sound system. Explain to the children how the disciples were afraid when Jesus showed up after they thought he was dead and buried. Continue telling the story of this

Resurrection appearance. Do they think Jesus would have been hungry after he was supposed to be dead? The disciples thought that they were seeing a ghost, but the "ghost" wanted something to eat. The disciples shared with him a piece of broiled fish. Share your broiled fish with all the children. Listen to their answers as they try to understand why the resurrected Jesus would want something to eat.

This incident cannot be wrapped up in a neat little package and concluded, but sharing broiled fish will help the children continue down the road to Emmaus as they search for the risen Christ themselves. Allow the children to help everyone discover the meaning of this text. The resurrection of Jesus is a mystery that we cannot fully explain to either children or adults. We, as Christians, are called to tell the story while encouraging both children and adults to make their own faith decisions.

SENSES: *Hearing, sight, smell, taste, and touch*

FOURTH SUNDAY OF EASTER
LECTIONARY READINGS:
Acts 4:5-12
Psalm 23
1 John 3:16-24
John 10:11-18

TEXT: Acts 4:5-12

PREPARATORY POSTURE: Visit the local jail or prison. If possible, examine a cell from the inside.

EXPERIENCE: Ask a number of adults to confess their faith in Jesus Christ. After they do so, have the children bring them to a designated jail. Sitting behind the altar rails in many churches will give the perfect effect of being "behind bars." This playful endeavor may bring out the impact of what happened to Peter and John, but be careful not to give the impression that confessing one's faith is somehow bad or inappropriate. Prison is more than just a few minutes in time-out. Perhaps you want to put the minister in prison, too, as a symbol that God is with them even in prison. The background of the story of how Peter and John were put in prison with the healing of the man who could not walk in Acts 3 will help the children understand the entire story more fully.

SENSES: *Touch, hearing, and sight*

FIFTH SUNDAY OF EASTER
LECTIONARY READINGS:
Acts 8:26-40
Psalm 22:25-31
1 John 4:7-21
John 15:1-8

TEXT: John 15:1-8

PREPARATORY POSTURE: Do some yard work that you have been avoiding. Prune any bushes that need to be pruned.

EXPERIENCE: Prepare a bowl full of grapes and a long brown rope. Ask the children to grab onto the brown rope, and give one grape each to most of the children. Encourage them to reach out like branches, holding the vine in one hand and the fruit in the other. The children have become the branches, and the brown rope is the vine. Remind them how Jesus said, "I am the true vine, and my Father is the vinegrower. He removes every branch in me that bears no fruit. Every branch that bears fruit he prunes to make it bear more fruit." While the children hold on as branches on the vine, explain to them the purpose of pruning. First, remove the branches that are without grapes, those that have not borne fruit. Second, prune the fruit-filled vines by harvesting the grapes and getting the children to put their hands down. Ask those that have been removed from the vine if they think they can bear fruit without being connected to the vine. Reattach the fruitless children to the vine, and give all the children even more grapes. In some traditions, all the grapes would be gathered and crushed by an adult to be used as grape juice for Communion.

For large churches: A string of Christmas lights with a few bad bulbs could also represent the vine, the branches, and the fruit. On some strands, when one light goes bad, the other bulbs beyond it will not light. Remove the bad bulb and throw it away. Replace it with a good bulb so that the other bulbs may get power from the vine and light up. This concept is more representational than participational, but it may work better with a large group of children.

SENSES: *Hearing, sight, smell, taste, and touch*

SIXTH SUNDAY OF EASTER
LECTIONARY READINGS:
Acts 10:44-48
Psalm 98
1 John 5:1-6
John 15:9-17

TEXT: Psalm 98

PREPARATORY POSTURE: Write new words to a familiar hymn tune or sing your favorite hymn with all your heart! Make a joyful noise!

EXPERIENCE: This psalm cries for the children to participate in its joy. Children love to make noise, and here is their
chance. The text gives the noises of clapping hands, singing,
and playing instruments, the trumpet and the lyre. Explore
the joyful noises the children like to make. Laughing, cheer-
ing, whooping, and other noises that the children come up
with can be incorporated into a choral reading of the psalm.
Tell the congregation about the marvelous things that God
has done in your church and community. Let one child
make his or her joyful noise after each marvelous thing is
announced. End with everyone making a joyful noise to the
Lord in his or her own way. God's presence with us is not
something about which to keep quiet, but a great thing
about which to sing new songs and make joyful noises.

SENSES: *Hearing, sight, and touch*

ASCENSION OF THE LORD/SEVENTH SUNDAY
OF EASTER
LECTIONARY READINGS:
Acts 1:1-11/Acts 1:15-17, 21-26
Psalm 47/Psalm 1
Ephesians 1:15-23/1 John 5:9-13
Luke 24:44-53/John 17:6-19

TEXT: Acts 1:15-17, 21-26

PREPARATORY POSTURE: Read Acts 1:18-20 and
Matthew 27. Fill your pockets with thirty silver-colored coins;
dimes, nickels, and quarters will do. Take a walk in a field.
Find a tree and reflect on the two stories of Judas's death.

EXPERIENCE: Children will enjoy the opportunity to
pick an adult to be a part of their circle. Gather all the children in a circle.

For small churches: Call each of the children to the circle by name. Help them name the twelve disciples, and explain what happened to Judas. Explain the dilemma of choosing another disciple to replace Judas and how the disciples chose Matthias. Talk to the children about what it means to be on God's team of disciples. We can always pick others to join the team. Pray with them, "Lord, you know everyone's heart. Show us who to pick." Then let them vote on someone to become part of the circle. You could invite one person, and then another and another until everyone is called to join the circle and be a disciple.

For large churches: You may ask each child to pick one pew of persons to be disciples with him or her. Let the children go and stand by the pew or pews they have picked. Pray a prayer that all might become Jesus' disciples.

For children faced with choosing captains and teams in school, it might be instructive and insightful to discuss the feelings of Joseph called Barsabbas, also known as Justus, the would-be disciple who was not picked in Acts 1. Just because we are not picked does not mean we cannot contribute or we are worthless.

SENSES: *Touch, hearing, and sight*

DAY OF PENTECOST
LECTIONARY READINGS:
Acts 2:1-21
Psalm 104:24-34, 35*b*
Romans 8:22-27
John 15:26-27; 16:4*b*-15

TEXT: Acts 2:1-21

PREPARATORY POSTURE: Take a ride on a roller

coaster or drive your car up and down a hilly road with the windows down.

EXPERIENCE: Take the children on an imaginary roller coaster ride with the rush of a violent wind, lots of ups and downs, and sharp curves. Riding a roller coaster is exciting, but it can also bring fear and apprehension. Compare this to the way the disciples felt at Pentecost. Electric fans and numerous candles could be used to create the Pentecost environment with the sound like a rush of a violent wind and divided tongues as of fire. The images themselves are similes, using *like* and *as,* so the idea is not to explain the fire and wind away, but to experience the fire and wind as they did at Pentecost. Adults have enough difficulty understanding the Holy Spirit, so we should not expect children to readily make the connection between wind, fire, and spirit. This idea attempts to re-create the experience of the first Pentecost, not as a substitute for the Holy Spirit, but as an invitation to the Holy Spirit to be present in the remembrance.

Another idea: Assign each child a group of people to represent: Parthians, Medes, Elamites, residents of Mesopotamia, and so on. Let them pick persons in the congregations to help them represent the groups until everyone in the congregation is included. Whenever the Acts text is read or the various groups are referred to in the sermon, the representatives are to stand. When the text is fully read, all the persons in the congregation should be standing, and the feeling of being gathered together in one place should be present once again. End the service with the reading of the Acts text, and have all return to their own homes and countries to spread the good news.

SENSES: *Touch, hearing, and sight*

TRINITY SUNDAY
LECTIONARY READINGS:
Isaiah 6:1-8
Psalm 29
Romans 8:12-17
John 3:1-17

TEXT: Isaiah 6:1-8

PREPARATORY POSTURE: Find a pair of tongs and a piece of ice. Touch the ice to your lips. Read the Isaiah passage, and if you feel led, pray a prayer of confession, asking for guilt to depart and your sin to be blotted out. Try to answer for your own life the question God is asking: "Whom shall I send, and who will go for us?"

EXPERIENCE: Read the first seven verses from the Isaiah text to the children. Then take a pair of tongs out and ask the adults for volunteers for some unknown task, implying that the tongs will be involved. Adults will be characteristically slow to respond. Then ask the children for volunteers. Hands will shoot up, and the children will struggle to be chosen even after hearing about the text about lips and live coals. Children will almost always respond faster and more freely than adults.

Give the tongs to an adult volunteer and let him or her pick up an ice cube and touch it to the lips of the children, saying, "Now that this has touched your lips, your guilt has departed and your sin is blotted out." Ask the rhetorical question, "Whom shall I send, and who will go for us?" The servant of the Lord responds as the children already have by volunteering (albeit with a different grammatical structure), "Here am I; send me." Now, let the children repeat together, "Here am I; send me."

SENSES: *Hearing, taste, touch, and sight*

PROPER 4

SUNDAY BETWEEN MAY 29 AND JUNE 4 INCLUSIVE

LECTIONARY READINGS:
(If After Trinity Sunday)
1 Samuel 3:1-10 (11-20)
Psalm 139:1-6, 13-18
2 Corinthians 4:5-12
Mark 2:23–3:6

TEXT: Mark 2:23–3:6

PREPARATORY POSTURE: Bake a loaf of bread and share it with friends. (You do not have to pluck the grain yourself.)

EXPERIENCE: In years past, society more clearly delineated the things that were permissible on the Sabbath and the things that were not. To animate the concept of a Sabbath, a day of rest, ask the children to pretend it's Monday morning. Instruct the children to run in place as you take them through the events of the day (for example, breakfast, teeth brushing, going to school, and so forth). Keep them running in place while running through every day in the week, highlighting the major events. Then on Sunday, let them rest. Did they need a day of rest? We all do. Discuss what Jesus did on the Sabbath and how it made the Pharisees angry. Help the children decide things that should and should not be done on the Sabbath.

SENSES: *Hearing, touch, and sight (Smell might come into play if you make them run long enough!)*

PROPER 5

SUNDAY BETWEEN JUNE 5 AND JUNE 11 INCLUSIVE

LECTIONARY READINGS:
(If After Trinity Sunday)
1 Samuel 8:4-11 (12-15), 16-20 (11:14-15)
Psalm 138
2 Corinthians 4:13–5:1
Mark 3:20-35

TEXT: Psalm 138

PREPARATORY POSTURE: Take a walk through the midst of trouble in your community. Every community has its trouble spots.

EXPERIENCE: Many children will have just finished school and will be dreaming of things to do during the summer. They will certainly be thankful that school is out or about to finish. Psalm 138 is a thanksgiving for God's getting someone out of trouble, and children will understand giving thanks for that. Help the children make a written list of things for which they are thankful using the acrostic style of poetry. Let them repeat together, "I give thanks, O Lord, with my whole heart for something beginning with *A*." Continue the repetition the whole way through the alphabet if time allows.

SENSES: *Hearing and sight*

PROPER 6

SUNDAY BETWEEN JUNE 12 AND JUNE 18 INCLUSIVE
LECTIONARY READINGS:
(If After Trinity Sunday)
1 Samuel 15:34–16:13
Psalm 20
2 Corinthians 5:6-10 (11-13), 14-17
Mark 4:26-34

TEXT: 1 Samuel 15:34–16:13

PREPARATORY POSTURE: Go to the store and try on a new pair of shoes, or try to fit into either an old pair of your shoes or the shoes of a family member.

EXPERIENCE: Ask the children to remember with you the Cinderella story. Let them help you retell the story. (I have always wondered why the glass slipper didn't change back at midnight, and the prince tried the shoe on people who didn't even look like Cinderella.) Then move to the anointing of David and retell that story from 1 Samuel. Take time to introduce the characters of Samuel, Saul, and Jesse. Carefully explain the significance of anointing. Let the children know the relationship between David and Jesus. The wicked stepsisters are strikingly similar to David's older brothers because they, too, are passed over for positions of royalty. David, like Cinderella, is busy working and not present to be chosen until the very end. Measure the children's feet with a glass slipper or shoe of some kind. Crown the youngest child king or queen, or crown all the children as part of God's kingdom. Cardboard crowns may sometimes be supplied by some fast food restaurants, or may be made by hand. No one is too young or insignificant to be called by God.

Another idea: In the Corinthians passage, walking by faith can be animated using blindfolds.

SENSES: *Hearing, touch, and sight*

PROPER 7

SUNDAY BETWEEN JUNE 19 AND JUNE 25 INCLUSIVE
(If After Trinity Sunday)
LECTIONARY READINGS:
2 Samuel 17:57–18:5, 10-16
Psalm 133
2 Corinthians 6:1-13
Mark 4:35-41

TEXT: Mark 4:35-41

PREPARATORY POSTURE: Go on a boat ride.

EXPERIENCE: Invite the children to join you in a boat either real or imaginary. A wooden boat makes an excellent focal point during worship this Sunday. Have the choir improvise to make the sounds of the wind, using microphones if necessary.

Instruct the congregation in a rain chorus.

Begin with the congregation slapping their hands on their legs slowly and softly.

Shift one-fourth of the congregation to snapping their fingers a bit more rapidly.

Shift a different one-fourth to tapping the backs and sides of the pews even faster.

Shift yet another one-fourth to clapping their hands as fast as they can.

Rock and sway back and forth in the boat with the children. At the climax of the wind, rain, and rocking, have someone walk up to the boat and calm the storm.

The wind and the sea obey Jesus. Discuss with children whom they obey.

SENSES: *Hearing, touch, and sight*

PROPER 8

SUNDAY BETWEEN JUNE 26 AND JULY 2 INCLUSIVE
LECTIONARY READINGS:
2 Samuel 1:1, 17-27
Psalm 130
2 Corinthians 8:7-15
Mark 5:21-43

TEXT: Mark 5:21-43

PREPARATORY POSTURE: Touch someone in love.

EXPERIENCE: I have a friend who used to be obsessed with touching famous people. She proudly displayed her list of the celebrities she had touched. It did not matter that she never had any interaction with that person. For her, the touch was enough. The woman in today's pericope also believes a simple touch will be sufficient.

Although the children will not understand the nature of the woman's illness, they will comprehend the fact that she had been sick for more years than they have been alive. From their perspective, she was sick for a long time.

Familiarize yourself with the concept of Christian relics, bones, or possessions associated with Jesus or a saint. Children may not understand the concept of things from the past with certain curative powers, but they are familiar with "kissing things to make them better." They know that touch can make them feel better.

Children do have things in their lives that they are not supposed to touch. The cross on the altar may be one such item. Allow the children to touch something in the sanctuary that they perceive is untouchable. Touching the cross in the sanctuary can be a powerful thing for adults as well. The children's sermon might be an invitation for all to come and feel the healing power of the cross for their lives. The children are unable to touch Jesus' garments, but many of them desire to touch the garments the minister wears. This would be a good Sunday to let them touch the minister's robe and stoles while answering the children's questions about the significance of each.

SENSES: *Hearing, sight, and touch*

PROPER 9

SUNDAY BETWEEN JULY 3 AND JULY 9 INCLUSIVE
LECTIONARY READINGS:
2 Samuel 5:1-5, 9-10
Psalm 48
2 Corinthians 12:2-10
Mark 6:1-13

TEXT: Mark 6:1-13

PREPARATORY POSTURE: Visit a number of homes in your community whose residents you do not know.

EXPERIENCE: Put the children in pairs. If there is an odd

number, invite an adult to complete the sets. Ask the children what kinds of things they would need to take with them for a long trip. Recall that Jesus sent his disciples out and told them to take no bread (for example, food), no bag (for example, suitcases, book bags, pocketbooks, and so forth), and no money. They could take a staff, sandals, and the clothes they were wearing. Provide a staff and sandals for the children to touch and see.

Send the children out two by two to share the good news around the congregation in the form of hugs or handshakes. When they return to the front, have a Welcome Mat where they can stamp and "shake the dust off their feet," especially if their hugs and handshakes have been rejected. Remind the children that Jesus tells his disciples not to turn around and come home when they are not welcomed. They are to shake the dust off their feet and go on.

Make a special note of Jesus' brothers' names for the children. James, Joses, Judas, and Simon are the four mentioned. His sisters' names are never stated. Many children do not realize that Jesus had brothers and sisters. Ask them what it would be like to be one of Jesus' brothers or sisters. Some questions might include: "What would it be like to have Jesus for a big brother?" "Would you get along better with your brothers and sisters if you treated them like they were Jesus?"

SENSES: *Hearing, touch, and sight*

PROPER 10

SUNDAY BETWEEN JULY 10 AND JULY 16 INCLUSIVE
LECTIONARY READINGS:
2 Samuel 6:1-5, 12*b*-19
Psalm 24

Ephesians 1:3-14
Mark 6:14-29

TEXT: Ephesians 1:3-14

PREPARATORY POSTURE: Write a letter to your church after the example of the letter Paul wrote to the church at Ephesus.

EXPERIENCE: The Ephesians text tells us that those who heard the word of truth and believed in God were marked with a seal of the promised Holy Spirit. Have enough Post-Its for the entire congregation in a small church or for all the children in a large church. Write the word *DISCIPLE* on each note. Then instruct the children to *mark* each person (or each child) in the congregation by placing a Post-It on them. Post-It notes stick just enough, just as Jesus stuck with the disciples and sticks with us, but it is relatively easy to get rid of the mark if we do not consciously strive to retain it. God marks us as God's children. Jesus marks us as his disciples.

SENSES: *Hearing, touch, and sight*

PROPER 11
SUNDAY BETWEEN JULY 17 AND JULY 23 INCLUSIVE
LECTIONARY READINGS:
2 Samuel 7:1-14*a*
Psalm 89:20-37
Ephesians 2:11-22
Mark 6:30-34, 53-56

TEXT: Ephesians 2:11-22

PREPARATORY POSTURE: Make a phone call to someone who lives far away. Bring the person near to you with your words.

EXPERIENCE: The Ephesians text tells us that those who were once far off have been brought near by the blood of Christ. Grover, one of the Sesame Street characters, has a patter that animates the idea of near and far. When the word *near* is spoken, he moves close to the camera. When the word *far* is spoken, he moves away from the camera. His patter goes on to include *around*, *over*, *under*, and *through*. For the purposes of the children's sermon, when the word *near* is spoken, have everyone try to get nearer to everyone else. When the word *far* is spoken, have everyone move away and scatter. The question then becomes, "How do we bring back someone who is far?" Let the children decide. Suggestions might include calling that person to come back, sending someone after that person, and finally having everyone move to where that person is, an incarnational approach, if you will.

Try placing a child in a wagon at one end of the church, far from the children's sermon spot. Using a red rope tied to the wagon, let the other children pull that wagon back to being near. The red rope is a symbol of the blood of Christ that brings us all near to God.

SENSES: *Hearing, touch, and sight*

PROPER 12

SUNDAY BETWEEN JULY 24 AND JULY 30 INCLUSIVE
LECTIONARY READINGS:
2 Samuel 11:1-15
Psalm 14

Ephesians 3:14-21
John 6:1-21

TEXT: Ephesians 3:14-21

PREPARATORY POSTURE: Jump as far as you can from
a standing position.

EXPERIENCE: Ask, "Who in the congregation is able to
kneel?" Some. "Who is able to pray?" All. "Who can jump fifteen feet?" None? Tell the children you can jump fifteen feet.
The children will not believe you. Let some of the children try
jumping that far. Call two of the biggest men in the congregation to come down to where the children have gathered.
Jump into their arms and let them carry you the fifteen feet.
Then carry some of the children across that distance. By ourselves we are not able, but with God and the help of others,
we are able to do so much more than we could by ourselves.

SENSES: *Hearing, touch, and sight*

PROPER 13

SUNDAY BETWEEN JULY 31 AND AUGUST 6
INCLUSIVE
LECTIONARY READINGS:
2 Samuel 11:26–12:13*a*
Psalm 51:1-12
Ephesians 4:1-16
John 6:24-35

TEXT: John 6:24-35

PREPARATORY POSTURE: Drive around your area and look for signs pointing to God's houses of worship.

EXPERIENCE: John is a book of signs that point us to who Jesus is. Both of these exercises use signs to tell us more about God.

1. Make a number of road signs for the children to hold, or have the children make the signs in Sunday school. Use *Stop, Yield, No Parking, Slow—Church Zone, Ten Miles to (your church name),* and so on. Ask them to read the signs and tell you what the signs mean or point to. Then hold up your sign, which is in the shape of the cross. To what does the cross point? Jesus' life, teaching, death, and resurrection all point us toward God.

2. Make a number of signs with the words *This Way to God* and an arrow. Have all the arrows facing in different directions, -> v ^. Give the children the signs to hold and ask, "Who is right?" "God is everywhere" should be the conclusion.

SENSES: *Hearing, touch, and sight*

PROPER 14

SUNDAY BETWEEN AUGUST 7 AND AUGUST 13 INCLUSIVE
LECTIONARY READINGS:
2 Samuel 18:5-9, 15, 31-33
Psalm 130
Ephesians 4:25–5:2
John 6:35, 41-51

TEXT: Ephesians 4:25–5:2

PREPARATORY POSTURE: Play a game of Pig or Horse on a local basketball court. The game consists of one person making a basket and the next person attempting to imitate the successful shot. If the first person misses, the second may choose how to make the next shot. When a player misses, the person receives a letter, and when the name of the game is spelled out, the person loses. Practice your best impersonation.

EXPERIENCE: Do your best imitation/impersonation for the children. See if they can guess who you are imitating. Let the children share their imitations with the congregation. Some of them will probably at least be able to imitate animals. If none of them have any or theirs have been exhausted, ask them to imitate things that you do. Lead them through a number of motions and sounds. Encourage them to imitate you. (I know one young lady who delights her brothers and sisters by imitating my preaching when she is in her bathrobe at home.)

When we imitate someone, it can be either flattering or derogatory. Identify the children's imitations as helpful or hurtful. Parents are good people to imitate, but adults do some things that we would not want to imitate. Let the children cite examples of things we should and should not imitate. The text tells us to be "imitators of God." Discuss with the children what things they might do to imitate God.

SENSES: *Hearing and sight*

PROPER 15

SUNDAY BETWEEN AUGUST 14 AND AUGUST 20 INCLUSIVE
LECTIONARY READINGS:
1 Kings 2:10-12; 3:3-14

Psalm 111
Ephesians 5:15-20
John 6:51-58

TEXT: 1 Kings 2:10-12; 3:3-14

PREPARATORY POSTURE: Burn incense as you study the Scripture this week.

EXPERIENCE: Children will enjoy this story about a little child who becomes king. Many children have had to deal with the death of a parent, and this may be a Sunday to help one of those children discuss feelings of sorrow. David has just died and gone to sleep with his ancestors. The olfactory sense is seldom a part of the mainline Protestant worship service. Allow the children to imitate Solomon, not by sacrificing, but by burning incense in a high place in the sanctuary, lifting a pleasing smell to the Lord. Let the children sit in the thronelike chair occupied by many preachers and recall with them Solomon's words. Ask the children, "What would you do if you were king or queen?" Solomon states, "I am only a little child; I do not know how to go out or come in." Solomon asks God to help him be a good king. God responds by saying some would have wished for money or long life or the death of their enemies, but Solomon just asks for God's help. Our prayers should also ask for God's help and not for things.

Parallels might be drawn to Simba's predicament in the Walt Disney film *The Lion King*. Upon the death of his father, Simba would have also been a child king. Not knowing what to do and being influenced not by God as Solomon is, but by his evil Uncle Scar, Simba runs away from his calling. God will help even little children fulfill their callings.

SENSES: *Hearing, touch, sight, and smell*

PROPER 16

SUNDAY BETWEEN AUGUST 21 AND AUGUST 27 INCLUSIVE

LECTIONARY READINGS:
1 Kings 8:(1, 6, 10-11), 22-30, 41-43
Psalm 84
Ephesians 6:10-20
John 6:56-69

TEXT: Ephesians 6:10-20

PREPARATORY POSTURE: Visit the local high school and ask to try on the protective gear that the football players wear.

EXPERIENCE: Ask the children, "Who is strong?" Then ask, "Who is strong in the Lord?" Acquire one or more football helmets and as many other pieces of a football uniform as possible. The football player and the hockey goalie wear modern armor with which the children will be familiar. Read the children the Ephesians text. Have them stand, and fasten a belt labeled truth around one child's waist. Help them with the shoulder pads as you recall the breastplate of righteousness. Use cleats or sneakers for shoes of peace. The shield of faith might be a water bottle to quench all the flaming arrows thrown at us. Let them all try on the helmet, reminding them of the helmet of salvation. Tapping the children lightly on the head and shoulders will show how the helmet protects them. Ask the one who is fully dressed in the gear, "Are you ready to go now?" The answer is no, for one piece is missing. They do not have the sword of the Spirit, the Bible. With the Bible as part of their armor, they are ready to face any battle.

SENSES: *Hearing, sight, and touch*

PROPER 17

SUNDAY BETWEEN AUGUST 28 AND SEPTEMBER 3 INCLUSIVE

LECTIONARY READINGS:

Song of Solomon 2:8-13
Psalm 45:1-2, 6-9
James 1:17-27
Mark 7:1-8, 14-15, 21-23

TEXT: Mark 7:1-8, 14-15, 21-23

PREPARATORY POSTURE: Wash your hands thoroughly with hot water and soap.

EXPERIENCE: Assemble a basin of warm water, a washcloth, some liquid soap, and a large towel. Invite the children to the front and tell them that Jesus' disciples didn't wash their hands before they ate. Children will love this fact; parents will hate it! Explain to the children that Jesus told the people who wanted his disciples to wash their hands, "It's not what's on the outside of people that hurts them, but what is in the heart." If there are dirty things in your heart, you can't wash them away with soap and water. Let the children decide on the things, such as hate and selfishness, that make our hearts dirty.

Wash and dry the children's hands to reemphasize this point. Send each child back to his or her seat when hands have been washed.

SENSES: *Hearing, touch, smell, and sight*

PROPER 18

LECTIONARY READINGS:
Proverbs 22:1-2, 8-9, 22-23
Psalm 125
James 2:1-10 (11-13), 14-17
Mark 7:24-37

TEXT: Mark 7:24-37

PREPARATORY POSTURE: Sweep up the crumbs under your kitchen or dining room table. Watch an entire television program without the sound.

EXPERIENCE: Read Mark 7:31-37 to the children. Talk with the children about what it means to be deaf or mute. Do they know anyone who cannot hear or speak? What would be the hardest things about not being able to hear? About not being able to speak? Explain what a disability is and how a person who is born without hearing might have trouble speaking. Point out how Jesus took the man aside in private, away from the crowd. Discuss why Jesus would have done that. Tell the children to put their fingers in their ears. Allow them to spit into their hands and touch their own tongues. Look up together, sigh, and then all yell, "Ephphatha." Also yell, "Be opened." Answer their questions about the story. Have them leave to tell others in the congregation, "Jesus has done everything well; he even makes the deaf to hear and the mute to speak."

SENSES: *Hearing, touch, taste, and sight*

PROPER 19

SUNDAY BETWEEN SEPTEMBER 11 AND SEPTEMBER 17 INCLUSIVE

LECTIONARY READINGS:

Proverbs 1:20-33
Psalm 19
James 3:1-12
Mark 8:27-38

TEXT: Mark 8:27-38

PREPARATORY POSTURE: Make a wooden cross, not one to be worn but one to be carried. Carry it a significant distance.

EXPERIENCE: Talk to the children about being measured. They will be eager to tell you how tall they are. Children have to be measured at amusement parks to see if they are able to ride certain rides. They have walls at home where they are measured. With a small group, measure each child's arms and legs as if for a suit or a dress. With a large group, measure a few children. Then measure an adult's arms and legs. Instead of giving the adult a suit or dress to wear, bring him or her a cross to carry out of the church. Give each child a pocket cross as a reminder that the cross was for children as well as adults. Repeat together Jesus' words: "If any want to become my followers, let them deny themselves and take up their cross and follow me."

SENSES: *Hearing, sight, and touch*

PROPER 20

SUNDAY BETWEEN SEPTEMBER 18 AND SEPTEMBER 24 INCLUSIVE

LECTIONARY READINGS:

Proverbs 31:10-31
Psalm 1
James 3:13–4:3, 7-8*a*
Mark 9:30-37

TEXTS: Mark 9:30-37; Psalm 1

PREPARATORY POSTURE: Walk through the sanctuary backward.

EXPERIENCE: Invite the children to the place that is opposite from where you usually meet in the church. Better yet, invite the adults forward for the children's sermon. Reverse all the things that are standard about your children's sermons. If you sit, stand. If you face the congregation, face the other direction. Then invite the children to join you in an exciting activity. Have them form a line. The biggest kids, by virtue of their size, will usually find their way to the front. Start the activity with them at the back of the line. Discuss the feelings of the ones who thought they were first as well as the ones who thought they were last. Try this at your next few children's activities in the church. After doing this at several events, the children in my church grew accustomed to the reversal. The older children moved to the back of the line in hopes of being moved to the front, so I stopped reversing the line.

SENSES: *Hearing, sight, and touch*

PROPER 21

SUNDAY BETWEEN SEPTEMBER 25 AND OCTOBER 1 INCLUSIVE

LECTIONARY READINGS:

Esther 7:1-6, 9-10; 9:20-22
Psalm 124
James 5:13-20
Mark 9:38-50

TEXT: Mark 9:38-50

PREPARATORY POSTURE: Closely examine your hands and then your feet. Stand in front of a mirror and look into your eyes. Reflect on times you have stumbled. Drink a glass of water.

EXPERIENCE: Have one or two pitchers of water and a number of cups available. You might want to place the cups and the water on the altar at the beginning of the service. When the children come forward, ask them to identify people in the congregation who bear the name of Jesus. Perhaps they could look for people with crosses or lapel pins. When people call themselves Christians, they are bearing the name of Jesus. Pour water into each cup and let the children distribute cups to the people they think bear the name of Christ. If time allows, give each of them a glass of water, too. (Be sure this activity occurs toward the end of the service or when the children leave for children's church if you give them each a full glass of water.)

The concept of deacon as servant, someone who would wait tables, as found in Acts 6 could be explained in conjunction with this experience.

SENSES: *Hearing, taste, sight, and touch*

PROPER 22

SUNDAY BETWEEN OCTOBER 2 AND OCTOBER 8 INCLUSIVE

LECTIONARY READINGS:

Job 1:1; 2:1-10
Psalm 26
Hebrews 1:1-4; 2:5-12
Mark 10:2-16

TEXT: Mark 10:2-16

PREPARATORY POSTURE: Pick up a child and hold him or her in your arms.

EXPERIENCE: Children understand what it means not to be included in an activity because they are too small. To animate this concept, get your ushers or other members of the congregation to control who comes forward for the children's sermon. Perhaps you want to have a height restriction, as they do at amusement parks, or an age restriction. Let the leader of the children's sermon stop these restrictions and invite all the children to come forward with no restrictions. Talk about how it felt to be excluded and the way Jesus included people, especially children.

For the risk taker: We often avoid the first half of this text with children, but today's children know more about divorce than we would like to admit. Sometimes divorce makes them feel cut off from the loving, caring, and safe arms of a parent they love. This might be a perfect day to let children talk about what it means to be married and how they feel about divorce.

SENSES: *Sight, touch, and hearing*

PROPER 23

SUNDAY BETWEEN OCTOBER 9 AND OCTOBER 15 INCLUSIVE

LECTIONARY READINGS:

Job 23:1-9, 16-17
Psalm 22:1-15
Hebrews 4:12-16
Mark 10:17-31

TEXT: Mark 10:17-31

PREPARATORY POSTURE: Review your last will and testament. If you do not have a will, make one. What must people do to inherit something from you?

EXPERIENCE: Tallest to shortest, oldest to youngest, alphabetical order—these are the orders with which children are familiar. Ask the children to order themselves from tallest to shortest. Start with the tallest and have them try to go through a small area where height makes a difference, a liturgical limbo, if you will. Here the last will be first and the first will be last. With the size limitations, you will also be able to discuss the camel going through the eye of the needle. (How about asking the children to line up richest to poorest?)

Another idea: Urge the children to try threading needles. (Tapestry needles have no sharp points.) After several attempts, show them a camel from a manger scene and talk about how hard it would be for even that camel to go through the eye of a needle. Let the children explore the statement "It is easier for a camel to go through the eye of a needle than for someone who is rich to enter the kingdom of God" (Mark 10:25).

SENSES: *Hearing, sight, and touch*

PROPER 24

SUNDAY BETWEEN OCTOBER 16 AND
OCTOBER 22 INCLUSIVE
LECTIONARY READINGS:
Job 38:1-7 (34-41)
Psalm 104:1-9, 24, 35c
Hebrews 5:1-10
Mark 10:35-45

TEXT: Mark 10:35-45

PREPARATORY POSTURE: Take a drive where there are traffic lights. When stopped at a red light, use the time constructively to pray for persons in your church. (My father used the bumps on his steering wheel as a sort of a rosary to remember his prayer concerns when waiting for the light to change.)

EXPERIENCE: Play Red Light, Green Light with the children, but add a new twist.

Game instructions: Line up the children on one side of the children's sermon area; turn away from them with your arms outstretched. Say "green light," and the children then move toward you. In the actual game, you would say "red light" to stop the action, but in this version, there are no red lights. Without a red light, the children will soon see the game is pointless, so switch to the way the game is usually played.

Leonard Sweet in *Homiletics Preaching Resource* suggests, "We are to respond to both signals, the ominous red lights of service and sacrifice (in Mark and Isaiah) and the hopeful green lights of salvation and redemption (Hebrews)."

SENSES: *Hearing, sight, and touch*

PROPER 25

SUNDAY BETWEEN OCTOBER 23 AND OCTOBER 29 INCLUSIVE

LECTIONARY READINGS:

Job 42:1-6, 10-17
Psalm 34:1-8 (19-22)
Hebrews 7:23-28
Mark 10:46-52

TEXT: Psalm 34:1-8 (19-22)

PREPARATORY POSTURE: Make or buy your favorite food and share it with a friend.

EXPERIENCE: Invite the children to take part in a taste test. First, ask the children how we know about God. Do we use our senses? Children have an idea of what God looks like, but what does God smell like? The psalter tells us to "taste and see that the LORD is good!" Prepare some foods that taste good to remind the children of the goodness of God. Let the children taste one thing they like and remind them that God has created all these good tastes for us.

SENSES: *Hearing, sight, touch, and taste*

PROPER 26

SUNDAY BETWEEN OCTOBER 30 AND NOVEMBER 5 INCLUSIVE

LECTIONARY READINGS:

Ruth 1:1-18
Psalm 146

Hebrews 9:11-14
Mark 12:28-34

TEXT: Mark 12:28-34

PREPARATORY POSTURE: Make a list of things you would like to see change in the church. Make a list of all the things you would like to change about yourself. Pray about where you can make a difference in the life of the church and in your own life.

EXPERIENCE: This Sunday is traditionally celebrated as Reformation Sunday. On October 31, 1517, Martin Luther wrote down Ninety-five Theses, ninety-five things he believed about the church. In Luther's time, the church sold indulgences that could be purchased to cancel out sins. Luther thought that forgiveness came through repentance, not purchases.

Give the children an example: Back in Martin Luther's day, if you did something such as hitting your sister, you could give the church ten dollars and God was supposed to forgive you. You never had to ask your sister for forgiveness. The money was supposed to buy you forgiveness from God.

Ask the children their opinion of this practice. Luther took his list and nailed it to the door of the church for everyone to see and read. That began a movement to improve the workings of the church, and the church was reformed based on many of Luther's ideas. Invite the children to help you make a list of the things that they believe about their church, including what they would like to see changed about the church. Let them all sign their names at the bottom. Allow them to nail or tape the list to the door of the church for everyone to see and read.

SENSES: *Sight and hearing*

PROPER 27

SUNDAY BETWEEN NOVEMBER 6 AND NOVEMBER 12 INCLUSIVE

LECTIONARY READINGS:
Ruth 3:1-5; 4:13-17
Psalm 127
Hebrews 9:24-28
Mark 12:38-44

TEXT: Mark 12:38-44

PREPARATORY POSTURE: Take a walk by a local bank, and find a spot from which to observe people going in and out of the bank. Look at the expressions on their faces, and hypothesize about the transactions they have just made. Try not to look suspicious!

EXPERIENCE: Sit the children in a strategic place in the sanctuary so they can watch the offering being taken up, or let the children actually take up the offering. Talk with them about what expressions they saw as people gave. Do the people look happy or sad? Ask the children what they think Jesus would want them to do with the money collected. Give each child a coin, but not necessarily the same size coin, and let them decide what they would like to do with their "mite."

SENSES: *Hearing, sight, and touch*

PROPER 28

SUNDAY BETWEEN NOVEMBER 13 AND NOVEMBER 19 INCLUSIVE

LECTIONARY READINGS:
1 Samuel 1:4-20
1 Samuel 2:1-10 or Psalm 16
Hebrews 10:11-14 (15-18), 19-25
Mark 13:1-8

TEXT: Hebrews 10:11-14 (15-18), 19-25

PREPARATORY POSTURE: Take a leisurely bath and wash your body with *pure water*. Close your eyes as you lay beneath the warm water and think about having your heart sprinkled clean from an evil conscience.

EXPERIENCE: The text speaks of having the law of God in our hearts and written on our minds. Explain to the children that during weekday morning prayer, the Jewish male actually wears the law of God on his forehead. *Phylacteries,* black leather cases containing scripture passages from the Torah, are held in place on the arm and forehead by black leather straps. Ask the children if they know any of God's laws. They will probably be most familiar with the Ten Commandments. (My daughter came up with, "Don't use bad manners.") Have modern phylacteries in the form of headbands available for each child with the words *"God's Law"* or one of the commandments written upon them. (Be prepared to answer questions about adultery!) A computer might even allow you to condense the entire Ten Commandments onto a piece of paper to be attached to the headband. Encourage the children to wear their headbands for the rest of the day, so that others might know these children want God's law written on their minds. (Pray for osmosis.) Remind the children that they will not learn God's laws by wearing them on their foreheads, for they cannot read their own foreheads. They will learn God's laws by reading God's Word.

Note: Jews do not wear phylacteries on holy days or

on their Sabbath, for these days are supposed to also be reminders of God's law.

SENSES: *Hearing, sight, and touch*

PROPER 29

SUNDAY BETWEEN NOVEMBER 20 AND NOVEMBER 26 INCLUSIVE
(Last Sunday After Pentecost or Christ the King)
LECTIONARY READINGS:
2 Samuel 23:1-7
Psalm 132:1-12 (13-18)
Revelation 1:4b-8
John 18:33-37

TEXT: 2 Samuel 23:1-7

PREPARATORY POSTURE: Get up early and watch the sunrise. Run your hand through the dew or the frost on the morning grass.

EXPERIENCE: Explain to the children that this text comes from the last words King David spoke before he died. After some discussion of the nature of last words, invite the children to pick up a prickly object such as a sweet gum pod, a rose stem, or a cactus leaf. The text tells us that "the godless are all like thorns that are thrown away; for they cannot be picked up with the hand" (v. 6). It is almost as though these things are saying, "Don't pick me up!" Ask the children what they would do if they did not want to be picked up. In our last days, we will want God to pick us up with God's loving hands. Ask the children, "What things might we do that will make us hard for God to pick up?"

Note: Do not get bogged down in making the connections to God picking us up. The purpose here is for the children to experience the metaphor and then draw their own conclusions.

SENSES: *Touch, hearing, and sight*

NOTES ─────────────────────

1. Sam Matthews, "Learning Like Children," *Wesleyan Christian Advocate*, 9 September 1994, p. 5.
2. Carolyn C. Brown, *Gateways to Worship* (Nashville: Abingdon Press, 1989), p. 8.
3. William Armstong, *Five Minute Sermons to Children* (New York: The Methodist Book Concern, 1914), p. 6.
4. David Elkind, *The Hurried Child* (Reading, Mass.: Addison-Wesley, 1981), p. 97.
5. Leander Keck, *The Church Confident* (Nashville: Abingdon Press, 1993), p. 104.
6. Dick Murray, *Teaching the Bible to Adults and Youth* (Nashville: Abingdon Press, 1987), p. 57.

SCRIPTURE INDEX – YEAR B ———